measure ONCE ™

Michelle Treese

Annie's®

A Note From the Designer

Knitting is the most perfect of hobbies. It is a skill that can be forever improved upon, it produces beautiful and useful objects, it connects us with women and men from all generations by allowing us to knit the same pattern and come up with the same product, and above all else, it is therapeutic. I usually have an advanced project and an easy project on the needles at any given time. The advanced project is for honing my skills and challenging my intellect. The easy project is meditative and relaxes me after a tough day.

Knitting also inspires incredible, and often manic, creativity that leaves me anxious to start something new and less anxious to knit the dreaded gauge swatch. We all know that this is essential for ending up with a well-fitting garment. It's hard to remember that knitting the gauge swatch will actually save time in the end when knitting the swatch itself sets you back a half hour or so from the beginning.

This book includes seven knitting patterns all using the same yarn. You will knit one gauge swatch before your first project and record your gauge information in the Get Your Gauge & Go! section on page 4. After that, you will be able to knit everything in the book with the same yarn and needles. Once your gauge information is recorded, you will be ready to grab your book, yarn and needles and knit without worry!

So go ahead and get started on that gauge swatch and enjoy doing so! After all, it will be the last time you need to for a while.

Happy knitting!

Michelle

Michelle Treese

Table of Contents

Williamsport, page 10

Barre, page 22

Largo, page 14

Get Your Gauge & Go!

For the patterns in this book, I used Cascade Yarns 220 Superwash wool and U.S. size 7 needles. Since every knitter's stitches vary in size due to the way that she tensions her yarn and holds her needles, you will need to determine which needle size will work best for you to come up with the following required gauge:

19 stitches and 26 rows in stockinette stitch = 4 inches

To get this gauge, I cast on 36 stitches and worked a few rows of garter stitch. Next, I worked 6 inches of stockinette with a 3-stitch garter border on each side, then I finished with a few more rows of garter stitch and bound off loosely. I cast on 36 stitches so that I would have a generous swatch to measure across, and the garter-stitch borders give stable, non-curling edges. Since we're only doing one swatch here, people, we had better do it right!

When you have your stockinette square, wash the swatch and block it without stretching. Then start by measuring for your stitch gauge. Place a pin somewhere on the left half of the square and place your ruler or tape measure below. Place another pin right at the 4-inch mark and remove the ruler. Now count the stitches between the pins. If you come up with more than 19 stitches between the pins, try a larger needle. If you have too few stitches, try a smaller needle. Keep adjusting the needle size until you come up with the required stitch gauge. Use the same method to measure your row gauge.

Once you get gauge, record the yarn and needle size in the Gauge Record table on page 5. There are a couple of extra spots in case you want to swatch more than one yarn. Later, when you want to knit something in this book, you'll just need to refer back to this page to know what yarn and needles to use!

I do realize there can be times when your knitting gauge may be slightly off. Let's face it, life happens, and any of the following conditions can affect the consistency of your stitches: when you're tired, cold, hot, excited, and the list goes on. Also, if you fill in the gauge section today and pick up the book again a few years from now, you may be a more experienced knitter and your gauge will be slightly different. Having said all of that, it might be a much better jumping-off point in your knitting to use a prior gauge measurement than no measurement at all. In other words, if you're like me, there will be times when you're going to cheat anyway, so you might as well cheat with some solid past information. Each pattern gives the gauge of the pattern stitch used in that project. After you've worked several inches of a project, measure the gauge to ensure that you're on target. ●

GAUGE RECORD

Date	Yarn	Needle Manufacturer & Material (e.g. metal, plastic or wood)	Needle Size

Acton

This is a simple and uniquely constructed cardigan without a single purl stitch.

· ·

Skill Level

◖■■□◗ EASY

Sizes

Woman's X-small (small, medium, large, X-large, 2X-large)
Instructions are given for smallest size, with larger sizes in parentheses. When only 1 number is given, it applies to all sizes.

Finished Measurements

Chest: 33 (38, 42, 46, 50½, 55½) inches (including front gap)
Length: 19¾ (20¼, 20¾, 21½, 22, 22½) inches

Materials

- Cascade Yarns 220 Superwash (worsted weight; 100% superwash wool; 220 yds/100g per skein): 5 (6, 7, 7, 8, 8) skeins each summer sky heather #1910 (A) and 1 skein aporto #856 (B)
- Size 7 (4.5mm) 29-inch circular needle or size needed to obtain gauge
- Size H/8 (5mm) crochet hook
- Removable stitch markers
- Stitch holders

Gauge

19 sts and 26 rows = 4 inches/10cm in St st.

17½ sts and 38 rows = 4 inches/10cm in garter st.

To save time, take time to check gauge.

Pattern Notes

Cardigan begins with a 1-piece sleeve/yoke section, which is worked from cuff to cuff. After sleeve seams are sewn, body stitches are picked up from the remaining yoke and worked down.

Mark public side (right side) of the fabric with removable marker.

Cardigan is worked back and forth in rows; a circular needle is used to accommodate the large number of stitches.

Sweater

Right Sleeve

With A, cast on 56 (60, 61, 63, 66, 68) sts.

Work 8½ inches in garter st, ending with a WS row.

Inc row (RS): K1, kfb, knit to last 3 sts, kfb, k2—2 inc sts.

Rep Inc row [every RS row] 20 (20, 22, 24, 25, 26) more times, ending with a WS row—98 (102, 107, 113, 118, 122) sts.

Mark both ends of last row for end of sleeve.

Yoke

Right Shoulder

Knit 40 (50, 58, 66, 74, 84) rows—shoulder should measure approx 4¼ (5¼, 6, 7, 7¾, 8¾) inches from markers.

Division row (RS): K43 (45, 47, 50, 52, 54) front sts, bind off 12 (12, 13, 13, 14, 14) sts for side neck, k43 (45, 47, 50, 52, 54) back sts.

Back Neck

Continue working back yoke while leaving front yoke sts at rest on needle.

Knit 1 WS row.

Dec row (RS): Ssk, knit to end—42 (44, 46, 49, 51, 53) sts.

Rep Dec row [every RS row] twice—40 (42, 44, 47, 49, 51) sts.

Beg and end with a WS row, knit 53 (55, 57, 59, 61, 63) rows—back neck measures approx 6 (6¼, 6½, 6¾, 7, 7¼) inches from bound-off neck edge.

Inc row (RS): Kfb, knit to end—41 (43, 45, 48, 50, 52) sts.

Rep Inc row [every RS row] twice, ending with a WS row—43 (45, 47, 50, 52, 54) sts.

Cut yarn. Back sts rem at rest on needle while front neck is shaped.

Right Front Neck
Rejoin A at neck edge of front yoke; knit 1 WS row.

Dec row (RS): Knit to last 2 sts, k2tog—42 (44, 46, 49, 51, 53) sts.

Rep Dec row [every 4 rows] once, then [every RS row] 4 times—37 (39, 41, 44, 46, 48) sts.

Beg and ending with a WS row, knit 11 (11, 13, 13, 15, 15) rows.

Bind off loosely.

Left Front Neck
With A and using long-tail method, cast on 37 (39, 41, 44, 46, 48) sts.

Knit 11 (11, 13, 13, 15, 15) rows.

Inc row (RS): Knit to last st, kfb—38 (40, 42, 45, 47, 49) sts.

Rep Inc row [every RS row] 4 times, then [every 4 rows] once, ending with a WS row—43 (45, 47, 50, 52, 54) sts.

Left Shoulder
Joining row (RS): K43 (45, 47, 50, 52, 54) front sts, cast on 12 (12, 13, 13, 14, 14) side neck sts, k43 (45, 47, 50, 52, 54) back sts—98 (102, 107, 113, 118, 122) sts.

Knit 41 (51, 59, 67, 75, 85) rows—shoulder should measure approx 4¼ (5¼, 6, 7, 7¾, 8¾) inches from Joining row.

Mark both ends of last row for end of yoke.

Left Sleeve
Dec row (RS): K1, ssk, knit to last 3 sts, k2tog, k1—96 (100, 105, 111, 116, 120) sts.

Rep Dec row [every RS row] 20 (20, 22, 24, 25, 26) more times—56 (60, 61, 63, 66, 68) sts.

Work 8½ inches even.

Bind off loosely.

Sew sleeve seams from cuff to markers.

Body
With RS facing and using A, beg at left front edge and end at right front edge, pick up and knit 1 st in

every ridge along yoke—approx 139 (160, 179, 196, 215, 236) sts.

Work 5½ inches in garter st, or until sweater measures approx 3 inches short of desired length, ending with a WS row.

Shape front edges as follows:

Dec row (RS): Ssk, knit to last 2 sts, k2tog—137 (158, 177, 194, 213, 234) sts.

Rep Dec row [every 4 rows] 5 times, then [every RS row] 3 times—121 (142, 161, 178, 197, 218) sts.

Bind off loosely.

Finishing
Weave in ends.

Block.

Body Edging
With RS facing, beg at center back neck and using A, work 1 rnd of sc evenly around edge of body. Join rnd with sl st and fasten off.

With B, work 1 sc in each sc of previous rnd. Join rnd with sl st and fasten off.

Sleeve Edging

With RS facing, beg at seam and using B, work 1 rnd of sc evenly around cuff. Join rnd with sl st and fasten off.

Single Crochet (sc)

Insert the hook in the second chain through the center of the V. Bring the yarn over the hook from back to front.

Draw the yarn through the chain stitch and onto the hook.

Again bring yarn over the hook from back to front and draw it through both loops on hook.

For additional rows of single crochet, insert the hook under both loops of the previous stitch instead of through the center of the V as when working into the chain stitch.

Single Crochet

Ties

With RS facing and using B and crochet hook, pull up a loop at yoke/body join of left front.

Work crochet chain for 12 inches or until tie measures desired length; turn.

Chain (ch)

Yarn over, pull through loop on hook.

Chain Stitch

Row 1: Sc in each ch across. Fasten off.

Rep on right front. ●

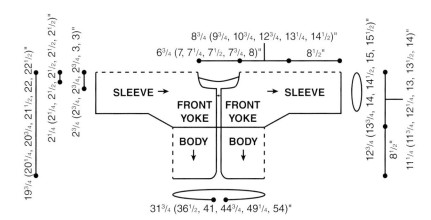

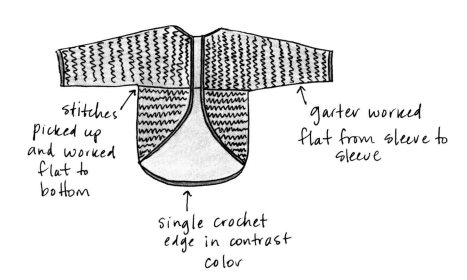

stitches picked up and worked flat to bottom

garter worked flat from sleeve to sleeve

single crochet edge in contrast color

Williamsport

This oversize cowl is easy to knit and perfect for snuggling with under your winter jacket.

Finished Measurements
Circumference: 30 inches (lightly blocked)
Length: Approx 13 inches

Materials
- Cascade Yarns 220 Superwash (worsted weight; 100% superwash wool; 220 yds/100g per skein): 2 skeins ridge rock #874
- Size 7 (4.5mm) 24-inch circular needle or size needed to obtain gauge
- Stitch marker

Gauge
19 sts and 26 rnds = 4 inches in St st.

15 sts and 32 rnds = 4 inches in Openwork pat.

To save time, take time to check gauge.

Pattern Stitches
2x2 Rib (multiple of 4 sts)
Pat rnd: *K2, p2; rep from * around.

Openwork (odd number of sts)
Rnd 1: K1, *yo, k2tog; rep from * around.
Rnd 2: *P2tog, yo; rep from * to last st, p1.
Rep Rnds 1 and 2 for pat.

Pattern Note
The cowl is worked in the round from the bottom up. There are more rounds of rib at the top so that cowl pulls in.

Cowl
Cast on 112 sts; mark beg of rnd and join, taking care not to twist sts.

Work 4 rnds in 2x2 Rib, and on last rnd, inc 1 st— 113 sts.

Work even in Openwork pat until piece measures 11 inches (unstretched), ending with Rnd 2 and on last rnd, do not work last yo—112 sts.

Work 11 rnds in 2x2 Rib.

Cut yarn.

Finishing
Weave in ends.

Block lightly. ●

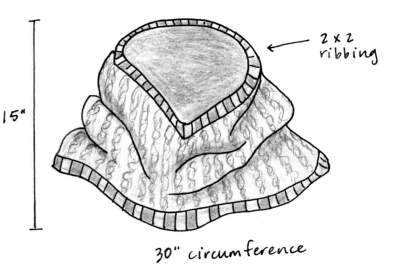

15"

2 x 2 ribbing

30" circumference

De Soto

This fun little purse is made with stockinette stripes embellished with crochet slip stitches that look like knitted stitches.

Skill Level
 EASY

Finished Measurements
12 inches wide x 6 inches tall, not including handles

Materials
- Cascade Yarns 220 Superwash (worsted weight; 100% superwash wool; 220 yds/100g per skein): 1 skein each ridge rock #874 (A), violet #805 (B), aporto #856 (C) and summer sky heather #1910 (D), or approx 100 yds A and 50 yds each B, C and D
- Size 7 (4.5mm) knitting needles or size needed to obtain gauge
- Size H/8 (5mm) crochet hook
- 1 fat quarter (18 x 22-inch piece of fabric)
- Thread to match fabric
- Sewing needle
- Pair of 6-inch circular bamboo handles

Embellishments
With A and crochet hook, loosely work sl st across last row of D. Fasten off.

With D, loosely work sl st across last row of C.

With C, loosely work sl st across last row of B.

With B, loosely work sl st across last row of A.

Weave in ends. Block.

Finishing

Lining
Iron fabric and cut to approx same size as knitted piece. Fold edges of fabric to the WS with 2 inches folded in on short sides and ½ inch folded in on long sides, then iron again. With WS tog, pin fabric to knitted piece positioned so that 2 inches of knitted fabric is uncovered on short sides and ½ inch is uncovered on long sides, then hand-sew fabric to knitted piece.

Gauge
19 sts and 26 rows = 4 inches/10cm in St st.

To save time, take time to check gauge.

Bag
With A, cast on 75 sts.

Working in St st, work 18 rows A, 17 rows B, 17 rows C, 17 rows D, 18 rows A.

Bind off.

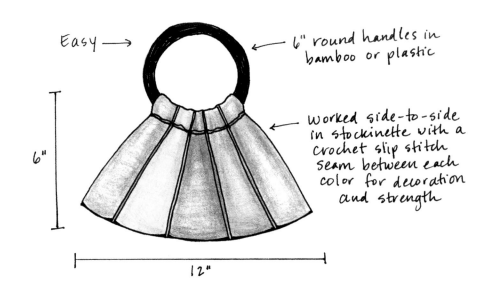

Easy →

← 6" round handles in bamboo or plastic

← Worked side-to-side in stockinette with a crochet slip stitch seam between each color for decoration and strength

6"

12"

Attach Handles

Wrap a short side around a handle; with RS facing, using crochet hook and A, sl st in place, making sure that all sts are in same row. Rep to attach other handle.

Slip Stitch (sl st)

Insert hook under both loops of the stitch, bring yarn over the hook from back to front and draw it through the stitch and the loop on the hook.

Slip Stitch

Fold piece in half with WS facing out. With crochet hook and A, work sl sts from bottom to approx 2 inches from handle to close side seam. Rep on other side. •

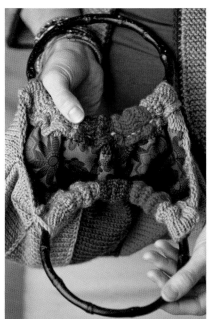

Largo

These cozy slippers knit up quickly. Plus, garter stripes are so much fun!

. . . .

Skill Level

 EASY

Sizes

Woman's small (medium, large)
Instructions are given for smallest size, with larger sizes in parentheses. When only 1 number is given, it applies to all sizes.

Finished Measurement

Length: 7¼ (7¾, 8½) inches—will stretch to fit 9 (10, 11) inches when on foot.

Materials

- Cascade Yarns 220 Superwash (worsted weight; 100% superwash wool; 220 yds/100g per skein): 1 skein each ridge rock #874 (MC) and violet #805 (CC)
- Size 7 (4.5mm) double-point needles (set of 5) or size needed to obtain gauge

Gauge

19 sts and 26 rows = 4 inches/10cm in St st.

17½ sts and 38 rows = 4 inches/10cm in garter st.

To save time, take time to check gauge.

Pattern Stitch

Garter Stripes (any number of sts)
Knit 2 rows MC, knit 2 rows CC.
Rep these 4 rows for pat.

Special Technique

3-Needle Bind-Off: With WS tog and needles parallel, using a 3rd needle, knit tog a st from the front needle with 1 from the back. *Knit tog a st from the front and back needles, then pass the first st over the 2nd to bind off. Rep from * across, then fasten off last st.

Pattern Notes

First a rectangle is knit that will form the toe of the slipper. Then the rectangle is folded in half (forming

the toe) and stitches are picked up on the other side and knit to form the back of the slipper. After the back seam is joined using 3-Needle Bind-Off and the side toe seams are sewn, a short edging is worked around the top.

Wool was used for this slipper because it is very elastic. Cotton or other inelastic yarn should not be substituted.

Toe

With MC, cast on 15 (15, 17) sts.

Work 15 (16, 17) reps of 4-row Garter Stripes pat, then knit 2 more rows with MC—31 (33, 35) garter ridges. Cut MC.

Back

Next row (RS): With CC, knit to the end of the row, then fold piece in half and with RS facing, pick up and knit 4 sts from cast-on edge, beg at nearest corner—19 (19, 21) sts.

Next row: Knit to end of row. Cut CC.

With RS facing and using new end of CC, pick up and knit in the first 4 cast-on sts at opposite corner, working from 4th st to corner, turn.

Next row: With CC, k4 sts just picked up—23 (23, 25) sts.

With RS facing, rejoin MC at new beg of row (first of the 4 picked up sts).

Continuing Garter Stripes pat, work 8 (9, 10) reps of 4-row pat—16 (18, 20) additional garter ridges, ending with a CC ridge.

Next row (RS): With MC, k10 (10, 11), k2tog, turn.

Fold piece in half with WS together; join halves using 3-Needle Bind-Off, forming back seam.

Finishing

Sew side seams of foot/toe.

Cuff Edge

With RS facing and using MC, pick up and knit 46 (50, 56) sts around the top edge; mark beg of rnd and join.

Knit 4 rnds.

Bind off firmly.

Weave in all ends. ●

Striped garter → in a long strip over toe, connected at foot opening, seamed on front sides and 3-needle bind off at heel

← border picked up at the end and stockinette worked in the round — border is tight so slipper stays on foot

Severn

Garter bumps in a contrasting color and funky buttons give this otherwise plain stockinette hat interest.

Sizes

Woman's small/medium (medium/large)
Instructions are given for smaller size, with larger size in parentheses. When only 1 number is given, it applies to both sizes.

Finished Measurement

Circumference: 20 (22) inches

Materials

- Cascade Yarns 220 Superwash (worsted weight; 100% superwash wool; 220 yds/100g per skein): 1 skein each of aporto #856 (A) and moss #841 (B)
- Size 7 (4.5mm) 16-inch circular and double-point needles (set of 5) or size needed to obtain gauge
- Stitch marker
- 2 (1-inch) buttons

Gauge

19 sts and 26 rows = 4 inches/10cm in St st.

20 sts and 25 rnds = 4 inches/10cm in Dashes pat.

To save time, take time to check gauge.

Pattern Stitch

Dashes (multiple of 10 sts)
Rnd 1: *K5 A, k5 B; rep from * around.
Rnd 2: *K5 A, p5 B; rep from * around.
Rnds 3 and 4: With A, knit.
Rnd 5: *K5 B, k5 A; rep from * around.
Rnd 6: *P5 B, k5 A; rep from * around.
Rnds 7 and 8: With A, knit.
Rep Rnds 1–8 for pat.

Hat

Brim

With A, cast on 110 (120) sts; mark beg of rnd and join, taking care not to twist sts.

Rnds 1 and 3: Knit.

Rnds 2 and 4: Purl.

Rnd 5: *K20 (22), k2tog; rep from * around—105 (115) sts.

Rnds 6–8: Rep Rnds 2–4.

Rnd 9: *K19 (21), k2tog; rep from * around—100 (110) sts.

Rnds 10–12: Rep Rnds 2–4.

Body

Change to Dashes pat; work [8-rnd rep] 4 (5) times, then rep Rnds 1–4 once more.

Crown

Note: Switch to dpns when sts no longer fit comfortably on circular needle.

Rnd 1: *K5 B, k3 A, k2tog A; rep from * around—90 (99) sts.

Rnd 2: *P5 B, k4 A; rep from * around.

Rnd 3: *K7 A, k2tog A; rep from * around—80 (88) sts.

Rnd 4: With A, knit.

Rnd 5: *K2 A, k2tog A, k4 B, k4 A, k4 B; rep from * to last 0 (8) sts, k2 A, k2tog A, k4 B—75 (82) sts.

Rnd 6: *K3 A, p4 B, k2 A, k2tog A, p4 B; rep from * to last 0 (7) sts, k3 A, p4B—70 (77) sts.

Rnd 7: With A, knit.

Rnd 8: With A, *k5, k2tog; rep from * around—60 (66) sts.

Rnd 9: *K3 A, k1 A, k2tog A, k3 B, k3 A; rep from * to last 0 (6) sts, k3 B, k1 A, k2tog A—55 (60) sts.

Rnd 10: *P3 B, k2 A, p3 B, k1 A, k2tog A; rep from * to last 0 (5) sts, p3 B, k2 A—50 (55) sts. Cut B.

Rnd 11: With A, *k3, k2tog; rep from * around—40 (44) sts.

Rnd 12: *K2, k2tog; rep from * around—30 (33) sts.

Rnd 13: *K1, k2tog; rep from * around—20 (22) sts.

Rnd 14: *K2tog; rep from * around—10 (11) sts.

Cut yarn, leaving a 6-inch tail. Using tapestry needle, thread tail through rem sts and pull tight.

Weave in all ends.

Block lightly.

Sew buttons to brim and lower body as shown in photo. ●

Sawgrass

The simple garter stripes add great texture to this short-sleeved, seamless, funky sweater.

Skill Level
 INTERMEDIATE

Sizes
Woman's small (medium, large, X-large, 2X-large)
Instructions are given for smallest size, with larger sizes in parentheses. When only 1 number is given, it applies to all sizes.

Finished Measurements
Chest: 37 (40½, 44, 48, 53) inches (buttoned)
Length: 27 (28½, 29¼, 29¾, 31¼) inches

Materials

- Cascade Yarns 220 Superwash (worsted weight; 100% superwash wool; 220 yds/100g per skein): 4 (5, 6, 6, 7) skeins moss #841
- Size 7 (4.5mm) 29-inch circular (or longer) and double-point needles (set of 5) or size needed to obtain gauge
- Stitch markers
- 2 (1-inch) buttons

Gauge
19 sts and 26 rows = 4 inches in St st.

19 sts and 30 rows = 4 inches in Garter Stripes pat.

To save time, take time to check gauge.

Pattern Stitch
Garter Stripes
Work 4 rows St st.
Work 2 rows garter st.
Work 4 rows St st.
Work 6 rows garter st.
Rep these 16 rows for pat.

Special Technique

1-Row Buttonhole: Work to button-hole position. Bring yarn forward, sl 1, bring yarn to back. [Sl 1, pass first slipped st over st just slipped, binding it off] 3 times. Slip the last st on RH needle back to LH needle; turn. Using the cable cast-on method, cast on 4 sts, turn. Sl 1, then pass last cast-on st over slipped st. Work to end of row.

Pattern Notes

This raglan cardigan is worked in one piece from the top down.

Slip the first stitch of every row purlwise.

Yoke

Cast on 74 (80, 88, 94, 100) sts.

Slipping the first st of every row pwise, knit 6 rows.

Set-up row (RS): Beg Garter Stripes pat and place markers as follows: sl 1, k15 (16, 17, 20, 19) left front sts, pm, k3 (4, 6, 4, 7) sleeve sts, pm, k36 (38, 40, 44, 46) back sts, pm, k3 (4, 6, 4, 7) sleeve sts, pm, k16 (17, 18, 21, 20) right front sts.

Next row: Sl 1, k4 (front band), purl to last 5 sts, k5 (front band).

Raglan Inc row (RS): Sl 1, *knit to 2 sts before marker, kfb, k1, slip marker, kfb; rep from * 3 times, knit to end—8 inc sts.

Maintaining garter-st bands and Garter Stripes pat throughout, rep Raglan Inc row [every 4 rows] 9 (9, 9, 8, 6) more times, then [every RS row] 12 (12, 11, 16, 20) times, ending with a WS row—250 (256, 156, 194, 316) sts, with 47 (48, 48, 54, 61) sts each sleeve.

Body Inc row (RS): Sl 1, *knit to 2 sts before marker, kfb, k1, slip marker, knit to marker, slip marker, kfb; rep from * once more, knit to end—4 inc sts.

Rep Body Inc row [every RS row] 1 (3, 6, 5, 7) more time(s), ending with a WS row—258 (272, 284, 318, 348) sts, with 40 (43, 46, 52, 55) sts each front and 84 (90, 96, 106, 116) back sts.

Body

Division row (RS): Removing raglan markers when you come to them, work front sts to marker; transfer sleeve sts to waste yarn; cast on 2 (3, 4, 4, 5) underarm sts, pm, cast on 2 (3, 4, 4, 5) underarm sts; work across back sts; transfer sleeve sts to waste yarn; cast on 2 (3, 4, 4, 5) sts, pm, cast on 2 (3, 4, 4, 5) sts, work to end—172 (188, 204, 226, 246) body sts.

Work 7 (13, 13, 13, 13) rows even.

Shape Waist

Dec row (RS): [Work to 3 sts before marker, ssk, k1, slip marker, k1, k2tog] twice, work to end—168 (184, 200, 222, 242) sts.

Maintaining pat as established, rep Dec row [every 6 rows] 8 (7, 6, 6, 6) times—136 (156, 176, 198, 218) sts.

Work 12 rows even.

Shape Hips

Inc row (RS): [Work to 2 sts before marker, kfb, k1, slip marker, kfb] twice, work to end—140 (160, 180, 202, 222) sts.

Rep Inc row [every 6 rows] 8 (9, 10, 9, 10) times then every 4 rows 1 (1, 0, 0, 0) time(s)—176 (200, 220, 238, 262) sts.

Work even (if necessary) until body measures 16 (17, 17, 17, 18) inches from underarms or approx 1¼ inches short of desired length, ending with a WS row.

Slipping first st of every row, knit 12 rows.

Bind off very loosely kwise.

Sleeves

Transfer sleeve sts from waste yarn to dpns.

Pick-up rnd: With RS facing and beg at center underarm, pick up and knit 2 (3, 4, 4, 5) sts, knit around sleeve, pick up and knit 2 (3, 4, 4, 5) sts to center underarm, pm for beg of rnd and join—55 (60, 64, 70, 81) sts.

[Purl 1 rnd, knit 1 rnd] 3 times.

Bind off very loosely pwise.

Button Strip

Cast on 7 sts.

Slipping first st of every row, work in garter st until piece measures 2½ inches, ending with a WS row.

Buttonhole row (RS): K2, work 1-Row Buttonhole over next 3 sts, k2.

Knit 3 rows.

Bind off.

Finishing

Weave in all ends.

Block to schematic measurements.

Securely sew end of strip without buttonhole to left front, approx 4 inches below neckline (see photo).

Sew button in center of strip on right front.

Sew button to left front band opposite strip. •

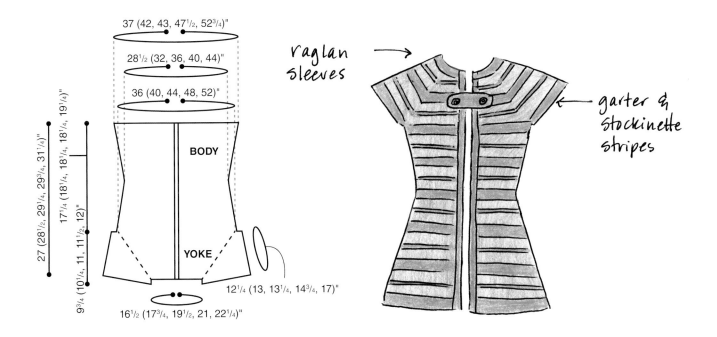

37 (42, 43, 47½, 53¾)"

28½ (32, 36, 40, 44)"

36 (40, 44, 48, 52)"

27 (28½, 29¼, 29¾, 31¼)"

17¼ (18¼, 18¼, 18¼, 19¼)"

9¾ (10¼, 11, 11½, 12)"

BODY

YOKE

12¼ (13, 13¼, 14¾, 17)"

16½ (17¾, 19½, 21, 22¼)"

raglan sleeves

garter & stockinette stripes

Barre

This stockinette, round-yoke cardigan is half one color and half another—perfect for stash busting!

Skill Level

◼◼◼◻ INTERMEDIATE

Sizes

Woman's small (medium, large, X-large, 2X-large)
Instructions are given for smallest size, with larger sizes in parentheses. When only 1 number is given, it applies to all sizes.

Finished Measurements

Chest: 35½ (39, 44, 47¼, 51½) inches (buttoned)
Length: 22 (23½, 24, 25, 25½) inches

Materials

- Cascade Yarns 220 Superwash (worsted weight; 100% superwash wool; 220 yds/100g per skein): 2 (3, 3, 3, 4) skeins each violet #805 (A) and strawberry pink #834 (B)
- Size 7 (4.5mm) 32-inch (or longer) circular and double-point needles (set of 5) or size needed to obtain gauge
- Stitch markers
- 7 (¾-inch) buttons

4 MEDIUM

Gauge

19 sts and 26 rows = 4 inches/10cm in St st.

To save time, take time to check gauge.

Pattern Stitch

Stripe Pattern
Worked in St st.
26 (30, 32, 34, 36) rows A
4 rows B
22 rows A
14 rows B
14 rows A
22 rows B
4 rows A
When Stripe pat is complete, continue with B to end.

Pattern Note

The body of cardigan is worked in one piece to the underarms. Sleeves are worked in the round to underarms, then joined with body, after which yoke is worked to the neck.

Body

With B, cast on 164 (180, 200, 220, 240) sts.

Row 1 (RS): K3, *p2, k2; rep from * to last st, k1.

Continue in established rib until piece measures 2 inches, ending with a WS row.

Change to A and Stripe pat.

Row 1 (RS): K40 (44, 49, 55, 58), pm, k84 (92, 102, 110, 124), pm, k40 (44, 49, 55, 58).

Work even until piece measures 13½ (14½, 14½, 15, 15) inches, ending with a RS row.

Next row (WS): *Purl to 4 (5, 6, 6, 7) sts beyond first marker; transfer 8 (10, 12, 12, 14) sts just worked to waste yarn for underarm; rep from * once, purl to end.

Set aside.

Sleeves

With dpns and B, cast on 60 (68, 72, 76, 80) sts; mark beg of rnd and join, taking care not to twist sts.

Work 6 rnds in 2x2 rib.

Change to A and St st; work even until piece measures 9 (9, 9½, 9½, 10) inches, ending 4 (5, 6, 6, 7) sts before beg of rnd.

Transfer next 8 (10, 12, 12, 14) sts to waste yarn for underarm, then transfer rem 52 (58, 60, 64, 66) sts to another piece of waste yarn for sleeve.

Cut yarn.

Rep for 2nd sleeve, but after transferring underarm sts to waste yarn, leave sleeve sts on dpns; cut yarn.

Yoke

Note: Continue Stripe pat until complete, then continue with B.

Joining row (RS): K36 (39, 43, 49, 51) right front sts, k52 (58, 60, 64, 66) sleeve sts, k76 (82, 90, 98, 110) back sts, k52 (58, 60, 64, 66) sleeve sts, k36 (39, 43, 49, 51) left front sts—252 (276, 296, 324, 344) sts.

Work 11 (13, 13, 15, 15) rows even.

Dec row (WS): P2, [p2tog, p4] 11 (13, 15, 12, 15) times, [p2tog, p3] 23 (23, 21, 35, 33) times, [p2tog, p4] 11 (13, 16, 12, 14) times, p2tog, p1—206 (226, 243, 264, 281) sts.

Work 11 (13, 13, 13, 15) rows even.

Dec row (WS): P1, [p2tog, p3] 11 (15, 15, 16, 18) times, [p2tog, p2] 23 (18, 21, 25, 23) times, [p2tog, p3] 11 (15, 16, 16, 19) times, p2tog, p1—160 (177, 190, 206, 220) sts.

Work 11 (11, 13, 13, 15) rows even.

Dec row (WS): P1, [p2tog, p2] 11 (15, 15, 16, 18) times, [p2tog, p1] 23 (18, 21, 25, 23) times, [p2tog, p2] 11 (15, 16, 16, 19) times, p2tog—114 (128, 137, 148, 159) sts.

Work 11 (11, 11, 13, 13) rows even.

Dec row (WS): [P2tog, p1] 11 (16, 15, 14, 16) times, [p2tog] 23 (15, 21, 31, 29) times, [p2tog, p1] 11 (16, 16, 14, 17) times, p2tog—68 (80, 84, 88, 96) sts.

Set-up row (RS): K3, *p2, k2; rep from * to last 5 sts, p2, k3.

Work 5 rows in established rib.

Bind off loosely in rib.

Finishing

Weave in ends.

Graft underarm sts using Kitchener st (see page 29).

Block.

Button Band

With RS facing and using B, pick up and knit approx 2 sts for every 3 rows along left front edge.

Knit 7 rows.

Bind off loosely.

Buttonhole Band

Mark positions for 7 buttonholes along right front edge, with first and last being ½ inch from top and bottom and the rest evenly spaced between.

With RS facing and using B, pick up and knit approx 2 sts for every 3 rows along right front edge.

Knit 2 rows.

Buttonhole row (WS): *Knit to buttonhole position, yo, k2tog; rep from * to last buttonhole position, knit to end.

Knit 4 rows.

Bind off loosely.

Block lightly.

Sew buttons to button band opposite buttonholes. •

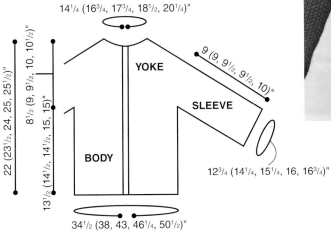

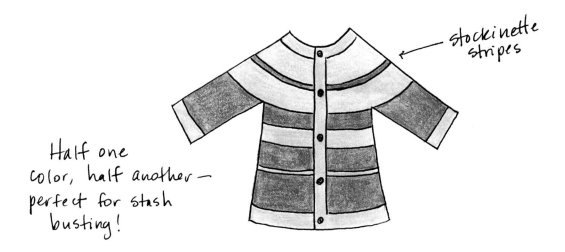

stockinette stripes

Half one color, half another — perfect for stash busting!

General Information

Abbreviations & Symbols

[ ] work instructions within brackets as many times as directed

( ) work instructions within parentheses in the place directed

** repeat instructions following the asterisks as directed

* repeat instructions following the single asterisk as directed

" inch(es)

approx approximately
beg begin/begins/beginning
CC contrasting color
ch chain stitch
cm centimeter(s)
cn cable needle
dec(s) decrease/decreases/ decreasing
dpn(s) double-point needle(s)
g gram(s)
inc(s) increase/increases/ increasing

k knit
k2tog knit 2 stitches together
kfb knit in front and back
kwise knitwise
LH left hand
m meter(s)
M1 make one stitch
MC main color
mm millimeter(s)
oz ounce(s)
p purl
p2tog purl 2 stitches together
pat(s) pattern(s)
pm place marker
psso pass slipped stitch over
pwise purlwise
rem remain/remains/remaining
rep(s) repeat(s)
rev St st reverse stockinette stitch
RH right hand
rnd(s) rounds
RS right side

skp slip, knit, pass slipped stitch over—1 stitch decreased
sk2p slip 1, knit 2 together, pass slipped stitch over the knit 2 together—2 stitches decreased
sl slip
sl 1 kwise slip 1 knitwise
sl 1 pwise slip 1 purlwise
sl st slip stitch(es)
ssk slip, slip, knit these 2 stitches together—a decrease
st(s) stitch(es)
St st stockinette stitch
tbl through back loop(s)
tog together
WS wrong side
wyib with yarn in back
wyif with yarn in front
yd(s) yard(s)
yfwd yarn forward
yo (yo's) yarn over(s)

Skill Levels

BEGINNER

Beginner projects for first-time knitters using basic stitches. Minimal shaping.

EASY

Easy projects using basic stitches, repetitive stitch patterns, simple color changes and simple shaping and finishing.

INTERMEDIATE

Intermediate projects with a variety of stitches, mid-level shaping and finishing.

EXPERIENCED

Experienced projects using advanced techniques and stitches, detailed shaping and refined finishing.

Standard Yarn Weight System
Categories of yarn, gauge ranges and recommended needle sizes.

Yarn Weight Symbol & Category Names	0 LACE	1 SUPER FINE	2 FINE	3 LIGHT	4 MEDIUM	5 BULKY	6 SUPER BULKY
Type of Yarns in Category	Fingering 10-Count Crochet Thread	Sock, Fingering, Baby	Sport, Baby	DK, Light Worsted	Worsted, Afghan, Aran	Chunky, Craft, Rug	Super Chunky, Roving
Knit Gauge Range* in Stockinette Stitch to 4 inches	33–40 sts**	27–32 sts	23–26 sts	21–24 sts	16–20 sts	12–15 sts	6–11 sts
Recommended Needle in Metric Size Range	1.5–2.25mm	2.25–3.25mm	3.25–3.75mm	3.75–4.5mm	4.5–5.5mm	5.5–8mm	8mm and larger
Recommended Needle U.S. Size Range	000 to 1	1 to 3	3 to 5	5 to 7	7 to 9	9 to 11	11 and larger

* **GUIDELINES ONLY:** The above reflect the most commonly used gauges and needle sizes for specific yarn categories.

** Lace weight yarns are usually knitted on larger needles and hooks to create lacy, openwork patterns. Accordingly, a gauge range is difficult to determine. Always follow the gauge stated in your pattern.

Inches Into Millimeters & Centimeters
All measurements are rounded off slightly.

inches	mm	cm	inches	cm	inches	cm	inches	cm
1/8	3	0.3	5	12.5	21	53.5	38	96.5
1/4	6	0.6	5½	14	22	56.0	39	99.0
3/8	10	1.0	6	15.0	23	58.5	40	101.5
1/2	13	1.3	7	18.0	24	61.0	41	104.0
5/8	15	1.5	8	20.5	25	63.5	42	106.5
3/4	20	2.0	9	23.0	26	66.0	43	109.0
7/8	22	2.2	10	25.5	27	68.5	44	112.0
1	25	2.5	11	28.0	28	71.0	45	114.5
1¼	32	3.2	12	30.5	29	73.5	46	117.0
1½	38	3.8	13	33.0	30	76.0	47	119.5
1¾	45	4.5	14	35.5	31	79.0	48	122.0
2	50	5.0	15	38.0	32	81.5	49	124.5
2½	65	6.5	16	40.5	33	84.0	50	127.0
3	75	7.5	17	43.0	34	86.5		
3½	90	9.0	18	46.0	35	89.0		
4	100	10.0	19	48.5	36	91.5		
4½	115	11.5	20	51.0	37	94.0		

Knitting Basics

Long-Tail Cast-On

Leaving an end about an inch long for each stitch to be cast on, make a slip knot on the right needle.

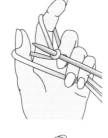

Place the thumb and index finger of your left hand between the yarn ends with the long yarn end over your thumb, and the strand from the skein over your index finger. Close your other fingers over the strands to hold them against your palm. Spread your thumb and index fingers apart and draw the yarn into a "V."

Place the needle in front of the strand around your thumb and bring it underneath this strand. Carry the needle over and under the strand on your index finger.

Draw through loop on thumb.

Drop the loop from your thumb and draw up the strand to form a stitch on the needle.

Repeat until you have cast on the number of stitches indicated in the pattern. Remember to count the beginning slip knot as a stitch.

Cable Cast-On

This type of cast-on is used when adding stitches in the middle or at the end of a row.

Make a slip knot on the left needle. Knit a stitch in this knot and place it on the left needle. Insert the right needle between the last two stitches on the left needle. Knit a stitch and place it on the left needle. Repeat for each stitch needed.

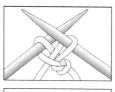

Knit (K)

Insert tip of right needle from front to back in next stitch on left needle.

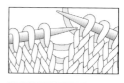

Wrap yarn under and over the tip of the right needle.

Pull yarn loop through the stitch with right needle point.

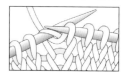

Slide the stitch off the left needle. The new stitch is on the right needle.

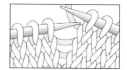

Purl (P)

With yarn in front, insert tip of right needle from back to front through next stitch on the left needle.

Wrap yarn around the right needle counterclockwise. With right needle, draw yarn back through the stitch.

Slide the stitch off the left needle.

The new stitch is on the right needle.

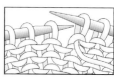

Pick Up & Knit

Step 1: With right side facing, working 1 st in from edge, insert tip of needle in space between first and second stitches.

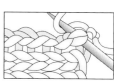

Step 2: Wrap yarn around needle.

Step 3: Pull loop through to front.

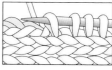

Step 4: Repeat Steps 1–3.

28

Increase (inc)

Two Stitches in One Stitch

Knit in Front & Back of Stitch (kfb)

Knit the next stitch in the usual manner, but don't remove the stitch from the left needle. Place right needle behind left needle and knit again into the back of the same stitch.

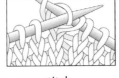

   Slip original stitch off left needle.

Purl in Front & Back of Stitch (pfb)

Purl the next stitch in the usual manner, but don't remove the stitch from the left needle. Place right needle behind left needle and purl again into the back of the same stitch.

   Slip original stitch off left needle.

Decrease (Dec)

Knit 2 Together (K2tog)

Insert right needle into next two stitches on left needle as to knit. Knit these two stitches as one.

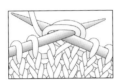

Purl 2 Together (P2tog)

Insert right needle into next two stitches on left needle as to purl. Purl these two stitches as one.

Bind-Off

Binding Off (Knit)

Knit first two stitches on left needle. Insert tip of left needle into first stitch worked on right needle and pull it over

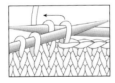

the second stitch and completely off the needle.

   Knit the next stitch and repeat. When one stitch remains on right needle, cut yarn and draw tail through last stitch to fasten off.

Binding Off (Purl)

Purl first two stitches on left needle. Insert tip of left needle into first stitch worked on right needle and pull it over the

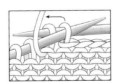

second stitch and completely off the needle.

   Purl the next stitch and repeat. When one stitch remains on right needle, cut yarn and draw tail through last stitch to fasten off.

Kitchener Stitch

This method of grafting live stitches together is often used for the toes of socks and flat seams. To graft edges together and form an unbroken piece of stockinette stitch fabric, divide all stitches evenly onto two knitting needles—one behind the other. Thread yarn into tapestry needle. Hold needles with wrong sides together and work from right to left as follows:

Step 1:

Insert tapestry needle into first stitch on front needle as to purl. Draw yarn through stitch, leaving stitch on knitting needle.

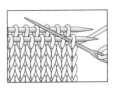

Step 2:

Insert tapestry needle into the first stitch on the back needle as to purl. Draw yarn through stitch and slip stitch off knitting needle.

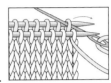

Step 3:

Insert tapestry needle into the next stitch on same (back) needle as to knit, leaving stitch on knitting needle.

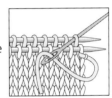

Step 4:

Insert tapestry needle into the first stitch on the front needle as to knit. Draw yarn through stitch and slip stitch off knitting needle.

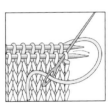

Step 5:

Insert tapestry needle into the next stitch on same (front) needle as to purl. Draw yarn through stitch, leaving stitch on knitting needle.

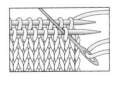

   Repeat Steps 2 through 5 until one stitch is left on each needle. Then repeat Steps 2 and 4. Fasten off. Grafted stitches should be the same size as adjacent knitted stitches.

Meet the Designer

Michelle Treese learned to knit and crochet as a child, but didn't discover her passion for it until she learned to read a pattern in 2007. That's when it all clicked, and she has been knitting obsessively ever since. She started designing in 2010 and has been published in both *Interweave Knits* and *Creative Knitting* magazines, along with having some self-published designs on Ravelry. Follow Michelle on her blog at www.michelletreese.com.

Special Thanks

Special thanks to Cascade Yarns for supplying the wonderful yarn for this book. All projects were made with Cascade Yarns 220 Superwash.

Cascade Yarns
1224 Andover Park E.
Seattle, WA 98188
(206) 574-0440
www.cascadeyarns.com

Photo Index

10

12

6

19

14

16

22

Measure Once is published by Annie's, 306 East Parr Road, Berne, IN 46711. Printed in USA. Copyright © 2013 Annie's. All rights reserved. This publication may not be reproduced in part or in whole without written permission from the publisher.

RETAIL STORES: If you would like to carry this pattern book or any other Annie's publications, visit AnniesWSL.com.

Every effort has been made to ensure that the instructions in this pattern book are complete and accurate. We cannot, however, take responsibility for human error, typographical mistakes or variations in individual work. Please visit AnniesCustomerCare.com to check for pattern updates.

978-1-59635-690-0

1 2 3 4 5 6 7 8 9